# HOW TO HAVE FINANCIAL CERTAINTY

# IN UNCERTAIN ECONOMIC TIMES

# (EVEN IF A CRASH COMES)

## WEALTH EXPRESS®

Copyright © 2024

All rights reserved.

ISBN-13: 979-8-9915448-1-8

## Also by Wealth Express®

The Freedom Protection Plan

For PERMANENT Financial Safety In
Financially Unsafe Times

Wall Street Is NOT Your Friend - *Watch Out!*

Don't Outlive Your Money!

This book is dedicated to your comfortable retirement.

You and I...We work hard. We love our country. We appreciate our loved ones. We do a pretty good job of saving money. We pay our dues. We dream of a nice retirement.

Imagine it...

The dream scenario...

You are FINALLY retired.

Busy schedule...gone.

Impatient boss, demanding customers...gone.

The Rat Race...gone.

Now it's good times, good friends, and 'goodbye' to decades of work, stress, and frustration.

Your days, now, are filled only with what you desire—traveling, relaxing, pursuing your passions. Living your American dream, no longer working for someone else's.

Feels good, right?

No more stress. No more struggle. No more money worries.

How GREAT…knowing you have plenty of money to continue living a rich and rewarding life through your golden years? Take a minute to let that feeling settle in because it is so sweet!

That's how retirement is *supposed* to feel.

Be honest. Is that what you'll be able to do in your golden years? Is that how you expect your retirement to go? More importantly, and this is a greater challenge…how do you ensure you have enough money to retire well in a very uncertain world? That…is one of the toughest problems to solve.

## Most people don't have the answer.

50% of Americans *expect to run out of money before they die*. Is that your current retirement trajectory?

You retire, thinking you can finally downshift and turn your attention to your family, your hobbies…relax! And then you start to see how much you can't afford. You see how prices keep going up. You hear about the market going down, again. You notice your retired friends doing things you don't have the money to do. You're forced to tell your spouse, 'we can't afford that'.

And it gets worse.

You have to cut back. You can't go out to dinner nearly as often or at all. You barely leave the house because you don't want to spend any money…and you're scraping together everything you have to keep the lights on to pay for your healthcare. How soon will it be before you start to pull money out of your investments—the same investments that are supposed to keep your retirement going? But you must because you need cash. You need money for day-to-day living. And you need the stress to go away.

But the stress doesn't go away. Does it?

Isn't it sad how long it takes to save money and how quickly those savings evaporate? Now what? Are you going to get a part-time job in retirement? Doesn't that defeat the whole purpose of retirement? But what else can you do? Right now, you have no money and no job.

And you're older. Historically, there's an age bias against hiring seniors despite their experience and expertise. Corporations like to trim the financial fat and hire lower-paid younger employees because they're perceived to have more energy and vitality…and they don't know any better. They don't know what they're worth.

But you do. And that stinks because now that you're older and retired, chances are you'll only be able to get a menial part-time job. Maybe it's greeting people at Walmart, collecting trays and wiping tables with a stinky, damp wash rag at the fast-food restaurant. Maybe you're bagging groceries.

Or maybe you'd like to avoid that altogether.

# INTRODUCTION

There is a surprisingly simple way to lock in guaranteed income that can NOT be reduced or decimated by new taxes or confiscated by anybody – not the US government, the IRS, state governments, or a lawsuit. It cannot be touched.

Why is this an issue? We live in a fantastic country, and times are good, right? Well, for starters, the economic devastations of COVID-related public policy are part of recent American history that's not far in the rearview mirror. So, this is no time for complacency.

## Because bad things can happen to good people at any time.

Do you know 20th-century American history? In 1933 FDR confiscated gold. Yes, this actually happened—if you don't believe me, Google it. And don't think for one second that the US Government can't confiscate your retirement savings, 401k, IRA, and whatever they deem as excess wealth. They'll even give you an IOU if you're lucky.

Not long ago, Greece froze citizens' bank accounts and levied an emergency tax on personal bank accounts with "too much money" in them.

If you think that Social Security can't be reduced—or means-tested and taken away from individuals with too much money or too many assets—you are probably kidding yourself. Medicare has already meddled with this.

As it is, over 75% of all bankruptcies experienced by seniors are due to medical emergencies and huge bills—hundreds of thousands of dollars in co-pays. One in five couples over age 60 find themselves financially destroyed by a medical crisis, illness, or infirmity that drains away ALL their savings! Keeping your money is NOT certain at all. That's why the "spend down, die broke" theory is so bad.

Perhaps you have friends who subscribe to this theory. Maybe it is working for them…so far. The rub is that this approach takes some world-class Swiss watch precision and accuracy to time things perfectly and magically foresee every eventuality and every financial challenge that arises in order for you to run out of money at the exact moment you run out of breath. Think your timing will be that perfect? Wanna put money on it? If that's how you approach savings and retirement, you have ALREADY bet money on it. That's a wager all Americans are highly unlikely to win. But…

## Good things can happen to good people <u>who plan</u>.

Back to the straightforward, surprisingly better way we first mentioned. What if there was a way to shield yourself from the financial pitfalls of this predictably unpredictable world? What if you could lay out a financial foundation that truly bolsters your retirement? Where you can do an end run around all the guesswork, eliminate the money worries that keep you up at night, and put all that fatiguing stress in the rearview mirror? You can.

THE FREEDOM PROTECTION PLAN® guarantees you lifetime income that absolutely cannot be snatched, confiscated, wealth taxed, or even reduced, ever, period. You can get the peace of mind you deserve and END WORRIES about running out of money and having to shrink your way of living, sell your home, or be a burden to your kids or family members –

PERMANENTLY, with this plan!

## Isn't Income For Life Just For Unsophisticated, Small Investors?

No, that's what the banks and the Wall Street financial advisors want you to think. Because they don't want you to have access to safe, secure, Guaranteed Income For Life. That requires none of their special handling as it generates reasonable returns and tax-deferred growth. To paraphrase the classic Cheap Trick song, Wall Street needs you to need them. They want YOU to pay for their expensive lifestyle. They want you not to have enough money, so you borrow money, so they can make money off the money you have to borrow. YOUR FINANCIAL SECURITY IS NOT IN THEIR BEST FINANCIAL INTEREST.

Guaranteed Income For Life plans are not unpopular plans amongst the Wall Street elite. They just don't like selling them, for the reasons mentioned above. Word is Warren Buffett secretly owns some Guaranteed Income For Life. More importantly, many knowledgeable, seasoned investors who use professional money managers and/or actively manage their diversified portfolios are SURPRISED AND IMPRESSED when they discover the truth about Guaranteed Income For Life. Most quickly see that it DOES have a place in their finances. If it works for them, it can work for smaller, less experienced investors.

## Can't I Do The Same Thing With Dividend-Paying Stocks?

We carefully analyzed publicly available portfolio data from one of the leading experts in high-yield investing, the editor of the #1 newsletter on the subject. Their portfolio holds 54 stocks and fund shares, all paying dividends. The overall yield in the past year was 7.3% (this was a GOOD year for the market). BUT. There are two flies in this ointment.

One. This rate is NOT guaranteed, is entirely variable and volatile, and requires hitting a bull's-eye every time—picking the right 54 stocks and allocating the correct percentage of your total capital to each. Personal honesty check: Can you pull that off? Can your financial advisor guarantee that? I doubt it! A different percentage allocation to these same stocks might have produced a 3%, 4%, or 5% yield. And if a BAD year hits, the returns become 2 or 3%, and the annual pay-out over your retirement might not average this 7%. Even worse, it might FALL. You might be forced to start saying things again like, "No, dear, we can't afford that!" OR this happens; the dividend holds but the value of the stock plummets by 20%, 30%, or 50%. So then what?

Two. Gains from dividend stock investing are all taxed now. IN COMPARISON, The Freedom Protection Plan® gives you an absolute guaranteed yearly %-yield that cannot fall—no matter what the market does—and some of it can be tax-free, and some tax-deferred. Your principal is NEVER at risk. Your NET, after-tax INCOME could be more from less and with ZERO risk—but only with the Freedom Protection Plan®.

The Freedom Protection Plan® is sophisticated. It's not complicated, risky, and does not require constant, worried oversight. You'll have time to do more of what you love to do instead of endlessly staring at screens and buying and selling.

You have a right to expect SAFETY. You deserve peace of mind and time to relax and enjoy life now. To know your standard of living is secure—for life. To have a lifetime "paycheck" arriving in your mailbox on schedule, guaranteed, for life. To give your spouse freedom from the anxiety of not having enough money. You EARNED this. You worked hard, played by the rules, raised a family, and saved responsibly. NOBODY should get to pull the rug out from under you now and steal the good life you've worked to create. NOBODY.

The best way to make this happen and be CERTAIN about your financial future is with a Guaranteed Income For Life Plan. But what exactly is it? And how does it create financial certainty in uncertain economic years ahead? How does it "crash"-proof your retirement? Read on…

**What if you could put financial certainty on your "done" list?**

**What if it was easy?**

**What if you COULD be certain?**

1

## The Problem: Retirement Uncertainty In Today's Economy

The status quo is never static. The only thing constant is change. Especially now. The pillars of stability–financial or otherwise– in this country continue to sink...NOTHING is certain. Except this. Guaranteed Income For Life. Because it's designed to float on the rising or falling financial waters…to always favorably change with the times.

## Financial Stability

You can't build a house without a solid foundation. That starts with the basics—understanding where you are and where you want to be…your situation, hopes, and dreams. Then, you craft a plan that will work for you. Not cookie cutter, not one-size-fits-all.

Having a clear understanding of your finances along with sustainable income streams you can count on during retirement allows you to maintain stability and security in your life. It enables you to budget and cover essential expenses, save and invest for the future, and readily weather unexpected financial challenges such as job loss or medical emergencies in the years leading up to retirement.

## Goal Achievement

Knowing where you stand financially at all times helps you set and achieve realistic financial goals. When you hit them consistently, year after year, you will start to realize your hopes and dreams. Whether it's buying a home, saving for retirement, or starting a business, having a solid financial foundation is essential. You must get this right as soon as possible to chart an intentional path, make informed decisions and course corrections, and take steps toward your retirement objectives.

## Reduced Stress

Financial uncertainty can lead to stress and anxiety, draining your energy and wreaking havoc on your mental and emotional well-being. Who needs that? The reality is that our money worries can adversely impact sleep and self-esteem. Feelings of anger, shame, and fear exacerbate pain and mood swings and fuel the risk of depression, anxiety, and unhealthy coping mechanisms. Being certain about your finances because of Guaranteed Income For Life can eliminate this stress, provide the peace of mind you deserve, and allow you to do more of what you love most.

## Improved Relationships

Financial stability and open communication about money are essential for healthy relationships, if it's with your spouse, family members, or friends. Money problems often put a strain on our relationships. Couples might fight more frequently or have trouble communicating. One spouse might feel they must constantly work to pick up the slack—and that means they don't have the margin to enjoy life outside of work.

Being certain about your finances is a massive benefit of having Guaranteed Income for Life. It enables you to manage joint finances effectively and avoid money conflicts. Enjoying your golden years with none of these conflicts will be fantastic. Others will wrestle with these debilitating tensions, but not you!

### Financial Independence

Knowing where your money is coming from and where it's going empowers you to make choices that support your financial independence. It allows you to take control of your financial future and reduces the possibility of having to rely on others for financial support. When you're in charge of your finances, you can make wise decisions about how to save money. You can choose how to save for retirement, build an emergency fund, or save for a major purchase like a house or a car. Financial independence means you never worry about where your next paycheck comes from. This puts you in control. Being in control feels good.

### Opportunity Readiness

Being certain about your finances puts you in a much better position to seize opportunities when they show up. Whether it's investing or starting a new business, firm footing makes a night and day difference. Imagine how it will feel to have the freedom to acquire that collectible car you've always wanted or take advantage of a career advancement opportunity! Imagine how great it would feel having financial clarity and certainty from Guaranteed Income For Life—so you can be confidently, decisively *pro*active, rather than being *re*active out of fear or frustration or panic.

## Adaptability to Change

Our world, our era, the financial markets, and the economy are constantly in flux—full of risk and instability. And things do seem to be getting worse, not better. Being certain about your finances gives you a clear advantage: the flexibility to adapt to changes no matter the circumstances, no matter the economy. Possessing that "edge" allows you to adjust your financial plan. You'll be able to navigate economic ups and downs with confidence. It gives you the breathing room to recognize and act on changes and to be good at learning how to do new things. Guaranteed Income For Life is flexible, agile…it is your untouchable "edge".

## What's Really Going On

Can you really be confident in anything in our

modern world? New Tech promises convenience, time savings, improved social connections, and simplicity while completely stripping privacy. And then there is password complexity, phishing, online account hacking, identity theft. Tech can be a nightmare. Politicians lie through their teeth to get what they want, and false promises are their #1 currency, designed to rob you of your currency.

Being certain about your finances is essential to achieve stability, reduce stress, and foster healthy relationships. But you can't be passive. You can't stick your head in the sand. You MUST do what's best for your family. When you do that and take charge, and get on the sure path with Guaranteed Income For Life, you'll find yourself in a position to pursue opportunities and plan for the future. Taking control of your financial destiny and building a secure and fulfilling life will feel awesome.

Because the past is prologue when it comes to the uncertain future…

## 2

# WHEN GOLD WAS CONFISCATED IN AMERICA!

During the Great Depression in the United States, President Franklin D. Roosevelt (FDR) signed Executive Order 6102 on April 5, 1933. This order required individuals and institutions to turn in most of their gold holdings to the Federal Reserve in exchange for paper currency at the rate of $20.67 per ounce. This action effectively nationalized gold and *made it illegal for private individuals to own significant quantities of gold coins, bullion, or certificates*.

There were several reasons behind FDR's decision to confiscate gold:

## Economic Crisis

The United States was in the midst of the Great Depression, which was marked by widespread unemployment, bank failures, and deflation in America and worldwide. FDR's administration sought to address the economic crisis and stabilize the U.S. financial system.

## Exchange Rate Stability

FDR and his economic advisors were concerned about maintaining the stability of the U.S. dollar and the exchange rate against foreign currencies. By removing gold from circulation and fixing the price of gold at $20.67 per ounce, they aimed to prevent currency speculation and maintain confidence in the dollar.

## Emergency Powers

FDR invoked emergency powers granted to the president under the Trading with the Enemy Act of 1917 to justify the confiscation of gold. While the act was originally intended for times of war, **it was interpreted broadly** to encompass the economic emergency of the Great Depression.

Just imagine! You've heard all the talk about the government trying to take your guns. But what if they actually tried (again) to take your gold? Your money!?? What if they 'interpreted' the laws OUT of your favor?

## Monetary Policy Flexibility

Confiscating gold gave the government greater control over monetary policy. It allowed them to expand the money supply by issuing more currency and implementing inflationary measures to stimulate economic activity and combat deflation. Government confiscation? In America? **It happened**, but can it happen again?

## Bolstering Confidence

FDR hoped that by centralizing gold reserves and utilizing government intervention, he could restore confidence in the banking system and the economy. The move was part of a broader strategy to reassure the public and stabilize financial markets during a period of unprecedented economic uncertainty.

## Gold Standard Abandonment

The confiscation of gold was a prelude to the eventual abandonment of the gold standard in the United States. In 1933, the U.S. government officially devalued the dollar and raised the price of gold to $35 per ounce, effectively abandoning the gold standard and allowing for greater flexibility in monetary policy.

Overall, FDR's decision to confiscate gold was a controversial and unprecedented measure aimed at addressing the economic challenges of the Great Depression. While it helped stabilize the financial system and restore confidence in the short term, it also raised concerns about government overreach and the erosion of individual property rights.

If the U.S. Government can decide to take gold….what does that mean for your savings? Surely that can't happen in the USA? …Or could it?….

3

# WHEN GREECE FROZE BANK ACCOUNTS

Greece froze bank accounts during the Greek financial crisis of 2015. This was part of a series of emergency measures implemented to prevent a collapse of the banking system and stabilize the country's economy. The decision to freeze bank accounts was a response to a severe liquidity crisis and the risk of a run on the banks, where depositors would rush to withdraw their funds en masse, potentially leading to bank failures and a complete breakdown of the financial system.

Several factors contributed to the decision to freeze bank accounts in Greece:

### Financial Instability

Greece had been grappling with a severe financial crisis for several years, characterized by high public debt levels, budget deficits, and economic recession. The crisis was exacerbated by Greece's inability to access international financial markets and borrow at affordable rates.

### Depositor Panic

Amid fears of a Greek exit from the Eurozone (dubbed "Grexit") and the potential return to the drachma currency, depositors rushed to withdraw funds from Greek banks, fearing that their savings would lose value or be converted into a weaker currency.

### Bank Runs

The surge in withdrawals led to liquidity shortages in Greek banks, making it increasingly difficult for them to meet depositors' demands for cash. There was a risk of widespread bank runs, which could have triggered a domino effect of bank failures and a collapse of the entire banking system.

## Capital Controls

To prevent a further drain on bank reserves and stabilize the financial system, the Greek government-imposed capital controls, including restrictions on cash withdrawals, transfers abroad, and the movement of capital. These measures aimed to limit the outflow of funds and restore confidence in the banking system.

Can you imagine? In this case, they're not taking your hard-earned money. But they're not letting you have it either. And that's the same as taking it.

## Negotiations with Creditors

The Greek government negotiated with international creditors, including the European Union, the International Monetary Fund, and the European Central Bank, to secure financial assistance and debt relief. The imposition of capital controls was seen as necessary to demonstrate Greece's commitment to implementing reforms and restoring fiscal stability. This is like the US government asking the Chinese to forgive half of the 770 billion in

Treasury securities they owe, which is 5% of the US national debt. Like that would ever happen! It's like getting the bank to give you a paid-in-full letter where they forgive the last 24 months of your 48-month car loans. Don't ever count on it!

## Social and Political Unrest

The financial crisis and austerity measures imposed by international creditors triggered social unrest and political instability in Greece. Freezing bank accounts was a way to maintain social order and prevent further economic turmoil while negotiations with creditors continued. What if they locked up your bank account money in the US? How would you pay bills? How would you survive?

The decision to freeze bank accounts in Greece highlighted the fragility of Greece's financial system and the challenges of managing a sovereign debt crisis within the Eurozone. If this scenario were to unfold here, why should your hard-earned savings be stolen to bail out government financial mismanagement? You love your country, but are you ready to make that kind of sacrifice? To forfeit any possibility of a good retirement?

If the government has a money shortage and

they can freeze your bank account...where will the money you need to live on come from?

4

# WHEN THEY FIDDLED WITH SOCIAL SECURITY

Social Security, established in 1935 as part of President Franklin D. Roosevelt's New Deal, has been a cornerstone of social welfare in the United States, providing retirement, disability, and survivor benefits to millions of Americans. However, over the years, there have been several notable occasions when the US government has made significant changes to Social Security, often sparking controversy and debate:

## 1983 Amendments

One of the most significant changes to Social Security occurred in 1983 when Congress passed the Social Security Amendments of 1983. These amendments included a series of reforms aimed at ensuring the long-term solvency of the Social Security system, <u>including raising the retirement age, increasing payroll taxes, and taxing some Social Security benefits.</u>

## 1996 Welfare Reform

In 1996, President Bill Clinton signed the Personal Responsibility and Work Opportunity Reconciliation Act (PRWORA), which made several changes to the welfare system, including provisions affecting Social Security Disability Insurance (SSDI) recipients. The law tightened eligibility criteria and imposed stricter work requirements for disability benefits.

## 2005 Debate Over Privatization

In 2005, President George W. Bush proposed a plan to partially privatize Social Security by allowing workers to invest a portion of their Social

Security taxes in private accounts. The plan faced strong opposition from Democrats and advocacy groups, and ultimately, Congress did not enact any significant changes to Social Security during Bush's presidency.

## 2010 Payroll Tax Cut

In 2010, President Obama signed a temporary payroll tax cut into law as part of the Tax Relief, Unemployment Insurance Reauthorization, and Job Creation Act of 2010. The law reduced the Social Security payroll tax rate from 6.2% to 4.2% for employees for the 2011 and 2012 tax years, intending to stimulate economic growth during the recession.

## 2021 Debate Over Social Security Expansion

In recent years, there has been debate over whether to expand Social Security benefits to address income inequality and provide greater financial security for retirees. Some politicians and advocacy groups have called for increasing benefits, raising the cap on taxable earnings, or implementing other reforms to strengthen the Social Security system.

Let's not forget that there is an entire industry of professionals—lobbyists, politicians, analysts, and so-called experts who wake up every day with the specific goal of ripping away your Social Security income. And that's IF Social Security doesn't run out of money first…<u>money you have already paid</u> towards retirement.

Point being…there's always someone ready to put your Social Security on the chopping block. If they take your Social Security away, or even if they slash it, how will you make up the difference?

# 5

## WHY THIS MATTERS

How many times have you eaten at a local fast-food restaurant and seen a delightful older woman in her seventies shuffling around the dining area, picking up food trays and wiping down tables? How many times have you gone to Walmart and been welcomed by a senior "greeter?" How many times have you gone to the grocery store and had your purchases bagged up by an older man who looks like they *should* be retired? Do you think they WANT to work there, or maybe they NEED to? It's very likely they MUST work there to make ends meet. Do you want that to be YOU? Are you willing to risk your golden years' stability and security on the whims of a gang of high-rolling lobbyists and their politician friends?

People are supposed to kick back and relax when they retire, and not face financial worries. However, when it comes to debt relief an increasing number of retirees are turning to bankruptcy. The mere mention of that dreaded word makes people over 65 cringe.

The world is in flux, more than ever. It has become absurdly, unforgivingly expensive...

Like any demographic group, retirees can face unforeseen financial challenges that may lead to bankruptcy. It's essential to understand the major causes of retiree bankruptcy and the negative outcomes associated with it. Tracing the graying American bankruptcy boom is not hard and involves factors like these...

### Medical Expenses

Skyrocketing healthcare costs are the new

normal. Spiraling out-of-pocket expenses for medications, treatments, and long-term care are a massive financial burden for retirees. It is especially rough for people with chronic health conditions or unexpected medical emergencies. High medical bills can deplete retirement savings and push retirees into bankruptcy. Are you willing to risk it, convincing yourself you'll miraculously dodge the healthcare bullet?

## Inadequate Retirement Savings

Many retirees may not have saved enough for retirement or have experienced investment losses that impact their financial security. Almost half of Americans don't have a dedicated retirement account, and 28% have <u>nothing</u> saved for retirement. Insufficient retirement savings can make it difficult for retirees to cover living expenses, leading to financial distress and potential bankruptcy.

Let's be honest. Most people fool themselves into thinking they have enough for retirement…

## Debt Accumulation

Many retirees carry debt into retirement, including mortgage, credit cards, or student loans. Servicing debt on a fixed income can strain retirees' budgets and make it challenging to meet other financial obligations, increasing the risk of bankruptcy.

## Job Loss or Income Reduction

Retirees who experience job loss, reduced work hours, or unexpected changes in income may struggle to make ends meet. A decrease in income can disrupt retirement plans and force them to draw down savings or rely on credit to cover expenses, potentially leading to bankruptcy.

## Pensions are Missing In Action

Pensions have all but disappeared for non-unionized workers, and those remaining are greatly underfunded and in danger of disappearing. This could leave pensioners destitute who are still relying on traditional defined benefit plans.

## Divorce or Family Obligations

Retirees who experience divorce or provide financial support to adult children or grandchildren may face additional financial strain. Divorce-related expenses, alimony, child support payments, or supporting adult children can impact retirees' financial stability and increase the risk of bankruptcy.

# The Tragic Result...

## Financial Instability

Don't kid yourself; bankruptcy plays no favorites. No matter what you wish for, when it calls your name, it can cost you all your assets, including your retirement savings, home, and personal belongings—leaving you financially vulnerable, needy, and uncertain about your future.

## Credit Damage

Bankruptcy can have long-lasting effects on retiree credit scores, making it difficult to access credit, secure loans, or obtain favorable interest rates in the future. Are you willing to bet you'll have enough time to recover from bankruptcy devastation in your golden years?

## Social and Emotional Impact

Bankruptcy places a heavy toll on your mental and emotional well-being, leading to stress, anxiety, depression, and feelings of shame or failure. For many people, this sadly becomes a downward spiral with no way of escape. Are you willing to gamble that you won't feel desperate if bankruptcy comes calling?

## Loss of Retirement Dreams

Bankruptcy will force you to downsize your lifestyle, delay altogether scuttle your retirement plans, or rely on family or government assistance for support. Do you honestly think bankruptcy won't destroy your retirement dreams and aspirations? It <u>can</u> happen to you.

## Time Is Running Out

Bankruptcy for retirees is no magic wand. Unlike someone who files bankruptcy in their mid-30s (with plenty of time for their credit score and investments to rebound after declaring bankruptcy), people in their mid-60s or older don't have enough time to get back on their feet.

And then, all of a sudden…you are picking up the fast-food trays, bagging the groceries, and saying "Welcome to Walmart". Not the retirement you had in mind.

## Limited Financial Options

Retirees who declare bankruptcy may have limited options for rebuilding their financial security, especially if they have depleted retirement savings or are unable to return to the workforce due to age or health reasons.

While bankruptcy is not the norm for retirees, it has become more prevalent among golden agers. Currently, 12.2% of all bankruptcies are filed by people 65 or older, and that number was just 2.1% in 1991. This alarming trend underscores the importance of careful financial planning, saving for retirement, managing debt, and maintaining adequate insurance coverage to protect against unforeseen circumstances in retirement.

You can't control what happens. You can only prepare.

**Call 833-600-2832 now**

**to schedule your FREE Retirement Risk Assessment Meeting with a Wealth Express® Certified Advisor.**

*WSA 123*

6

# THE CHANGING LANDSCAPE OF RETIREMENT

As people age, they often encounter various new, unforeseen challenges. Americans aged 60 and above are no exception. Some of the most common challenges faced by this group include:

## Financial Security

Many older adults face financial challenges due to retirement because of fixed incomes, rising healthcare costs, and potential unexpected expenses. Ensuring financial stability becomes more crucial than ever. Financial certainty is the foundational essence of Guaranteed Income For Life.

## Social Isolation

With changes in social networks, retirement from work, and loss of friends and family, older adults may experience loneliness and social isolation, which can negatively impact mental and emotional well-being.

## Housing and Accessibility

Finding suitable housing that is affordable, safe, and meets their changing needs can be challenging. Additionally, accessibility issues such as mobility limitations may arise, requiring modifications to living spaces. With Guaranteed Income For Life, you'll have the funds for your housing needs 100% dialed in.

## Caregiving

Older adults often become caregivers for their spouses or other family members, while others may require caregiving assistance due to declining health or disabilities. Balancing caregiving responsibilities can be beyond demanding. If this is you, and you're caught between caring for elderly parents and raising your younger children, keeping your eye on the retirement ball is almost impossible. With a Guaranteed Income For Life plan, that worry goes away. It provides a foundation upon which you can balance your dual priorities.

## The Importance Of Stability And Certainty In Retirement Planning

Turbulence is a daily part of aging. Instability is baked right into the recipe. But you CAN steady the ship…

Anything you can do to create stability is paramount in effective retirement planning and the wealth creation process. During retirement, having a stable income source like Guaranteed Income For Life directly impacts our financial security and peace of mind in the post-employment years. Here's a reality check on why stability is crucial:

### Income Reliability

Having regular, dependable income is essential

for living a simple, steady, SANE retirement. This includes covering basic living expenses, healthcare costs, and leisure activities—without the worry of sudden income fluctuations or loss of purchasing power.

## Long-Term Financial Security

Stable, well-crafted retirement planning like Guaranteed Income for Life helps safeguard against unforeseen financial emergencies or market downturns. It ensures you have enough funds to sustain their lifestyle throughout your retirement years, including during periods of economic volatility.

## Global Events

As you and I both know, global events can significantly negatively impact economic stability. Their potential to disrupt national economies, create uncertainty, and amplify risks is crucial. Here are some ways global events can adversely affect financial stability. It is good to bear these in mind, and also rest assured they will not affect you—because you'll enjoy a stable, smooth retirement income stream with your Guaranteed Income For Life plan.

## Trade Disruptions

Events out of your control such as trade disputes, tariffs, or geopolitical tensions can disrupt global supply chains, reduce international trade volumes, and hinder economic growth. During COVID, we saw first-hand how trade disruptions can lead to higher business costs, reduced consumer purchasing power, and increased market volatility. Are you willing to gamble that additional trade disruptions won't come home to roost in the USA? Guaranteed Income for Life gives you a tremendous hedge against that, just in case.

## Financial Market Volatility

Global events, such as geopolitical conflicts, natural disasters, or unexpected policy changes, can trigger volatility in financial markets. Sharp fluctuations in asset prices, exchange rates, or interest rates can disrupt capital flows and create instability in the financial system. Do you think you can magically avoid this kind of mayhem? Guaranteed Income for Life will shield you from all of it!

## Economic Uncertainty & Resource Shocks

Sadly, this topic is more than familiar…you just

lived through it. Uncertainty surrounding global events, such as elections, geopolitical tensions, or major public health crises, can disrupt supply chain and affect consumer and business confidence. This tension can lead to reduced spending, investment, and economic activity. Retirees who had Guaranteed Income for Life during the global COVID years experienced zero need to reduce spending because they still got their regular monthly paycheck, like clockwork. Global events have the potential to create significant economic instability. Policymakers, businesses, and investors must remain responsive to these international developments to mitigate their adverse effects.

Do you want to count on all those challenges being perfectly met and well handled by politicians and bureaucrats who DO NOT have your best interests in mind? Or that somehow these sweeping, destructive economic outcomes will never materialize? And if they do, that none of this will affect your investments?

Do you think that even the most well-meaning world leaders and economists have your best interests in mind? Think again. They are too busy campaigning and raising money for themselves.

## Risk Mitigation

By diversifying your investments and incorporating stable income sources such as pensions, Guaranteed Income For Life, and fixed-income securities, you can mitigate investment risks and reduce exposure to market volatility in your retirement years. This approach helps protect your retirement savings from significant losses and provides a buffer against fluctuations in asset values. You'll love how Guaranteed Income For Life bakes in the certainty you need.

## Peace of Mind

Knowing that your financial future is certain, secure, and well-planned brings tremendous peace of mind. Guaranteed Income For Life will allow you to focus on enjoying your retirement years without the stress of financial uncertainty or the need to worry about monitoring and adjusting your investment strategies constantly.

## Legacy Planning

Stability in retirement planning is also crucial in effective legacy planning. Solid planning ensures you can leave a financial legacy for your heirs or support charitable causes you care about most. Even better, if desired and with the right plan, your legacy can become multi-generational without compromising your financial security during retirement. Your secret weapon, your Wealth Express® Certified Advisor will help you get your arms around legacy planning, and you'll discover that it's not as complicated as you think. But more about that later in this book.

## Your Path To Stability And Certainty

In essence, stability through retirement planning provides the foundation for a financially secure and fulfilling retirement. Consistent planning allows you to confidently pursue your retirement goals and aspirations without undue financial stress or uncertainty. Guaranteed Income For Life will put you in the driver's seat, and anchor the stability you need to rock your dream retirement.

# 7

## The SOLUTION...Guaranteed Income For Life

Who would blame you if you're sitting there reading this and starting to feel all is lost, as if retirement is hopeless. Don't worry, there IS hope.

WHAT IF?....there is a financial plan that has your back, no matter what? One that is carefully crafted so that disruptions to global economies, mayhem from domestic or international politics, poorly designed monetary policy and economic uncertainty can never undermine your financial stability.

They are crafted to insure your way of living, for life. By trustworthy people who know that most retirement plans are spouted out by Wall Street types who want to line their wallets with your money and don't want you to know about Guaranteed Income For Life? Who intentionally make their retirement plan options massively confusing and so complicated you give up and sign where they put the sticky yellow Post-it notes?

There is hope! You can live a stable, secure, financially-free retirement—no matter who is in the Oval Office.

You can be prepared for the worst financial storms. You can make plans to protect your finances and secure a certain financial future. So you never have to worry about what's happening next.

You CAN lock in Guaranteed Income For Life with zero risk.

You CAN make your IRA or 401(k) market-proof.

You CAN get a solid paycheck every month, just like you always have before retirement.

You CAN avoid running out of money, enjoy time with the grandkids, travel, pursue new interests, and simply relax.

Guaranteed Income For Life offers a unique combination of security and growth potential, making it an attractive option for your retirement planning. Here's a summary of how it provides security and growth potential.

## Principal Protection

Guaranteed Income For Life provides hope because it uniquely protects your principal investment from market downturns. Unlike other plans that are directly tied to the performance of the underlying assets, Guaranteed Income For Life offers a minimum guaranteed interest rate. Imagine how that will feel, knowing you will be immune to market swings.

## Participation in Market Upside

In addition to providing principal protection, Guaranteed Income For Life can participate in market gains through indexed interest crediting strategies, where your plan's performance is linked to the performance of a stock market index, like the S&P 500. How often do you see that strategy working on your behalf with other retirement plans?

## Cap and Floor Mechanisms

Guaranteed Income For Life plans typically include cap and floor mechanisms. These limit the maximum potential interest credited and the minimum guaranteed interest rate. Sure, upside is limited…but it is also GUARANTEED. And that provides downside protection that protects your principal to give you peace of mind. Do your other investments offer this type of protection?

## Tax-Deferred Growth

Guaranteed Income For Life offers tax-deferred growth. This means that any interest earned is only taxed once it is withdrawn. You'll rest easy, knowing that annual taxes do not diminish your plan's earnings—and they compound and grow, enhancing your plan's overall performance. Plus, if you do your Guaranteed Income For Life investing inside your Roth IRA, you will have tax-free income after age 59 ½!

## Lifetime Income Options

In addition to providing growth potential, Guaranteed Income For Life can be structured to offer guaranteed lifetime income payments. This provides you with a reliable income stream to supplement your other sources of retirement income. That's the kind of enhanced financial security you can bank on throughout your retirement. On which you can be <u>certain</u>.

## Comparing Guaranteed Income For Life With Other Retirement Investment Options.

Here's what Guaranteed Income For Life does for you: It means you'll finally have an investment vehicle that fits your retirement intentions in a way that can be superior to other retirement options. For instance...

## Comparison With 401(k) Investment

401(k) plans offer tax-deferred growth and potentially employer-matching contributions, but they are subject to market volatility, leaving the principal vulnerable to losses during market downturns. Can you be certain your 401(k) will be immune to wild market swings?

Guaranteed Income For Life provides principal protection against market downturns while offering growth potential through indexed interest crediting strategies. This can give you more stability, peace of mind, and certainty—especially during market volatility.

## Comparison With IRA Investment

Like 401(k) plans, IRAs offer tax-deferred growth potential but also come with market risk and fluctuating account values.

Guaranteed Income For Life offers you the opportunity for growth linked to the performance of a specified stock market index while guaranteeing that the principal will not decrease even when there are market downturns. Where else will you find that kind of iron-clad protection? Will your financial advisor deliver these kinds of worry-free returns, no matter what? This invaluable retirement tool can offer you a fantastic balance of growth potential and security, particularly if you prefer to minimize risk in your retirement portfolio…and ensure that you won't have to spend every single day of your retirement staring at screens, charts, candles, and Bollinger Bands full time—hoping that you somehow get it right on your own and outsmart armies of Wall Street professionals.

## Comparison With Certificates of Deposit (CDs)

CDs offer a fixed interest rate and principal protection, but the returns may not keep pace with inflation. They also lack the potential for higher returns. Plus, buying power is based on your income after taxes. Remember that interest on CDs outside a qualified retirement plan is taxed as ordinary income. You've known forever that CDs are a great cash equivalent, but that's all.

Guaranteed Income For Life typically offers higher growth potential than CDs by linking interest crediting to the performance of a stock market index. While your retirement fund may not offer the same level of liquidity as CDs, Guaranteed Income For Life provides you with the opportunity for potentially higher returns. Remember, Guaranteed Income For Life still provides you with principal protection.

Performance + Protection. That's a combination that any forward-thinking, sober, retiree should find hard to resist. Then again, you and I know that common sense is not all that common. I suspect by the very fact that you are still with me and reading this that you DO have common sense, that you take retirement seriously, and that you are connecting all the dots…dots which lead you to the inevitable fact that…Guaranteed Income For Life should be an essential financial pillars supporting your financial future.

Guaranteed Income For Life offers you a compelling combination of principal protection, growth potential, and lifetime income options during retirement. Compared to other retirement vehicles such as 401(k) plans, IRAs, and certificates of deposit, Guaranteed Income For Life looks fantastic. With a balance of security and growth potential, Guaranteed Income For Life can play a valuable role in helping you achieve your long-term financial goals. Plus, it helps to maintain financial stability throughout retirement. Your Guaranteed Income For Life investments will stay steady like a rock while the rest of the financial world goes up and down.

**Call 833-600-2832 now**

**to schedule your FREE Retirement Risk Assessment Meeting with a Wealth Express® Certified Advisor.**

*WSA 124*

Because the next crash IS coming…

# 8

# UNDERSTANDING THE MARKET/FINANCIAL CYCLE

## Financial Crises

Historically, economic downturns or recessions have occurred for many reasons. Throughout our history, financial crises have been primary triggers of economic downturns. Examples include the Great Depression of the 1930s, caused by the stock market crash of 1929 and subsequent bank failures, and the 2008 global financial crisis, sparked by the collapse of the subprime mortgage market in the United States. It is important to know financial history, even if you think that past boom-bust cycles will not happen again. Here are three significant market crashes and their impact on financial markets.

## The Great Depression (1929)

The Wall Street Crash of 1929, also known as Black Tuesday, marked the beginning of the Great Depression. This was the most severe economic downturn in modern history.

Can you imagine living through that? Can you even fathom such a thing happening today? What would you do? What COULD you do? It's horrible to think about. But….who knows how far we really might have been from this during COVID? What if something far worse than COVID was unleashed in the USA or worldwide? The results could be a historically familiar echo of the Great Depression…in your lifetime!

The crash saw stock prices plummet, wiping out billions of dollars in wealth virtually overnight. Between 1929 and 1932, stock market values dropped by nearly 90%.

The economic fallout extended beyond the stock market, leading to widespread bank failures, massive unemployment, poverty, and a collapse in consumer spending. The Great Depression profoundly affected individuals and families, with many losing their life savings and facing extreme hardship.

Living through the Great Depression left indelible marks on those who went hungry, stood in bread lines, ate in soup kitchens—and learned to save string, foil, and rubber bands then and for the rest of their lives.

### The Dot-Com Bubble Burst (2000)

You'll no doubt recall the late 1990s and the rapid rise in internet-related companies. Fueled by investor speculation and optimism about the internet's potential, investment values skyrocketed, and fortunes were made.

However, by early 2000, many of these companies were overvalued. Reality came home to roost because the sky-high stock prices were detached from actual earnings and fundamentals.

When the dot-com bubble burst, stock prices for technology sharply declined. Many dot-com companies went bankrupt, and investors suffered significant losses.

The fallout from the dot-com bubble burst affected tech stocks and broader market indices. It led to a recession in the early 2000s and caused widespread job losses, particularly in the technology sector.

## The Global Financial Crisis (2007-2008)

The collapse of the subprime mortgage market in the United States triggered the global financial crisis. Risky lending practices and the securitization of subprime mortgages fueled this collapse. Because these money guys loooooooooooove taking chances with YOUR money.

The crisis led to a liquidity crunch. Financial institutions faced mounting losses on mortgage-backed securities and other complex financial instruments.

Major financial institutions collapsed or required government bailouts to prevent further systemic damage. Stock markets worldwide experienced sharp declines, with many indices losing more than 50% of their value. Did anyone bail you out back then when your portfolio plummeted and your dreams went down the drain? Not even!

The global financial crisis resulted in a severe

recession. Millions of people lost their jobs, there were widespread foreclosures, and consumer and investor confidence significantly declined. It took years for economies to recover fully from the effects of the crisis.

Did anyone learn their lesson from all of this? I doubt it. We're already hearing about bank regulation rollbacks, removing consumer guardrails…etc.

## Monetary Policy

Central banks use monetary policy tools, like interest rates to manage economic growth and inflation. Sometimes, to curb inflation or asset bubbles, central banks raise interest rates, which can lead to a slowdown in economic activity. Can you trust the Fed to always do what's in your best interest? Will they be sure to time their monetary policy moves on your behalf?

These next four topics might seem annoyingly over-academic….yet you can't escape them and their power to upset your lifestyle if you don't have the right retirement plan. Guaranteed Income For Life gives you a cushion against all of these! So, read on, be aware, and know you'll have peace of mind with Guaranteed Income for Life.

## Sound Fiscal Policy (Can You Rely On It?)

Government spending and taxation policies can also influence economic cycles. Austerity measures, involving reduced government spending can contribute to economic downturns by reducing aggregate demand.

## External Shocks

Wars, natural disasters, and geopolitical tensions can disrupt economic activity and lead to downturns. For example, the oil crises of the 1970s, triggered by conflicts in the Middle East, caused significant economic recessions in many countries.

## Technological Change (Can You Control It?)

Technological advancements can lead to structural changes in the economy. These may trigger temporary disruptions and downturns in certain industries. For example, shifting from traditional domestic manufacturing to moving the work offshore led to significant job loss in many sectors. Automation and digital technologies have also contributed to job losses, creating regional economic downturns. With Guaranteed Income For Life, having zero disruptions and steady income will feel fantastic, and there's no need to worry about your financial security.

## Asset Bubbles (Good to observe, knowing it can't touch you!)

Periods of rapid asset price appreciation, like we experienced in the housing bubble leading up to the 2008 financial crisis, can eventually burst. When a bubble ruptures it leads to economic downturns as asset values plummet and consumer confidence declines.

With Guaranteed Income For Life, you'll enjoy rock-solid assurances in the face of any economic downturns. Yes, economic downturns are a normal part of the economic cycle. Their severity and duration can vary depending on the underlying causes and policy responses. Governments and central banks often implement measures to mitigate the impact of downturns.

But can you count on politicians doing the right thing that somehow works in your favor? Do you want to depend on measures like fiscal stimulus packages, monetary easing, and regulatory reforms to stimulate recovery? With Guaranteed Income For Life, you'll have the financial certainty you need, and the regular income you desire—and these economic cycle issues can't hurt you.

# The Signs Of Economic Downturns And How To Spot Them Early.

## (What you want to monitor)

Since we are both responsible investors and the last time I checked, we are not full-time economists, here's a quick review I put together about some important things to keep your eye on—key indicators of an impending economic downturn.

## GDP Growth

A significant slowdown or contraction in Gross Domestic Product (GDP) growth is often a clear sign of an economic downturn. Government agencies release quarterly GDP reports to observe these trends.

## Unemployment Rate

Rising unemployment rates indicate a weakening labor market, which can lead to reduced consumer spending and economic activity. Monitoring unemployment claims and job creation trends can provide useful early warnings of an economic downturn. Of course, being retired generally means not having to work. And with a

Guaranteed Income For Life investment delivering your retirement paycheck month after month, you get all the perks of work without the daily grind, the hassle, and the commute.

## Consumer Spending

Consumer spending is a significant driver of economic activity. A decline in consumer confidence and spending can signal an impending downturn. Retail sales data and consumer sentiment surveys are helpful indicators to track. With Guaranteed Income for Life, you won't need to curtail your planned retirement spending, because it is already baked into the budget!

## Business Investment

Reduced business investment, reflected in declining capital expenditure and business confidence surveys, can indicate that firms are scaling back expansion plans due to economic uncertainty. You can easily find free, informative business confidence surveys online.

## Manufacturing Activity

Manufacturing activity often serves as a leading indicator of broader economic trends. A contraction in manufacturing output, as measured by indices such as the Purchasing Managers' Index

(PMI), can signal an economic downturn.

## Yield Curve Inversion

When short-term interest rates exceed long-term interest rates, it often indicates expectations of a future economic slowdown. This phenomenon, called yield curve inversion, has historically preceded many recessions.

## Corporate Profits

Declining corporate profits can suggest weakening demand and economic conditions. You can monitor corporate earnings reports and profit margins to get insights into the health of businesses and the broader economy.

Take a look around. Do you SEE things getting better? Are your friends feeling good and relaxed and liking how things are working out? Are you? Or is sentiment still down and dropping lower? Your defense against that can be a Guaranteed Income For Life plan.

To spot these indicators early, economists and policymakers regularly monitor various economic data and indicators. Utilizing advanced statistical models and econometric techniques, economists analyze historical trends. Do you want to count on nameless, faceless economists doing the right thing to protect your financial interests? With Guaranteed Income For Life, you have a plan that assures you can rest easy—no matter what the economic tea leaves say!

9

## The Elephant in the Room

I want to take a moment to tell you how we assemble your Freedom Protection Plan, and how we can help you to have Guaranteed Income For Life…so you don't run out of money before you die.

By far, the simplest, surest financial 'tool' for Guaranteed Income For Life is called an "annuity."

You may have heard criticism about this financial product, but most of it is unfounded, and, as with all criticism, just like Mom and Dad told us, we must "consider the source". Most criticism of annuities comes from Wall Street people and "financial advisors" who want your money being "actively managed" by them. That means they wanna use your money for buying and selling stocks, fund shares ETF's, even risky items like crypto…generating lush commissions and/or fees on every move and every trade, day by day. This puts your money at risk. Because money stays safely at rest inside annuities, providing you with guaranteed monthly income, they don't like it!

However, very recently, Larry Fink, CEO of Blackrock, one of THE largest money management firms on Wall Street, a manager of billions of dollars of pension funds, <u>shocked the world by coming out IN FAVOR OF ANNUITITES</u> – even presenting his new plan for remaking 401k accounts and pension accounts to automatically transition into individually held annuities, paying – you guessed it! – GUARANTEED lifetime income, with a "paycheck" every month.

To be fair, annuities do have "a catch", and I'll get to that in just a minute or two.

If I may first, just a little history. Annuities are financial contracts that can be traced back to ancient Rome. Back then, annuities were known as "annuals" that provided a stream of income for life that the person could not outlive, in exchange for an up-front payment. The word 'annuity' comes from the Latin "annua", which simply means 'annual payments'. A common use of annuities was to guarantee the pensions of safe, lifetime income for the Roman soldiers. In a way, annuities were invented to take care of their retired military veterans.

In the 1600's, European governments started using annuities. In the 1700's the British Parliament approved sale of annuities – and rich Europeans flocked to these 'safe harbors'. In the U.S., annuities have been available for more than TWO CENTURIES. Actually, Social Security is a government-issued annuity, guaranteeing lifetime income. Although, unfortunately, Congress has stolen its funds so its survivability as-is is in question as early as 2026. However, the life insurance industry's annuities are extremely well-funded and well-administered.

Could be why in 2023 Americans invested more than 385 BILLION dollars in annuities. A record high.

People just like you rely on their annuity payments, whether only as the solid foundation supporting other, more diversified investments, or as their entire retirement 'safe harbor'. Either way, their check arrives every month.

Today, annuities are issued and backed by giant, rock-solid life insurance companies. And they're used around the globe for sound financial planning, for secure retirement, avoidance of risk of loss and certain income.

Today, there is a variety of annuities that we choose from, for your personalized Freedom Protection Plan. Some have fixed pay-outs, some offer limited upside opportunity tied to markets along with a "buffer' against downside risk, some start monthly income immediately, some have a delay period to accumulate interest and raise monthly pay-out, and most have time "windows" where you can withdraw funds without penalties (unlike most CD's).

Annuities can be TAX-ADVANTAGED, so that you LEGALLY have more tax-free retirement income. This might sound complex, but we make it simple for you, so you get exactly the financial results you want. Your Plan is built to match your goals and needs. And incidentally, Wealth Express® is INDEPENDENT, not captive to any one insurer. We 'shop' for you and for your Plan.

In many ways, figuring out your Medicare, Medicare plan B, C, D, Medicare Advantage options, choices and best plan for you is similar to figuring out your Freedom Protection Plan. In developing your personal Freedom Protection Plan, we consider everything you tell us about your finances and needs and goals, and we identify the best annuities to fit perfectly. There is NO confusion.

Now, about "the catch". You purchase annuities. In doing so, you trade that one-time, up-front amount for the guaranteed lifetime income, but the original principal (premium payment) is no longer yours; it belongs to the annuity issuer, a large insurance company. You buy your guaranteed lifetime income stream. You can call that "a catch" if you want, but it actually isn't. There's nothing sneaky or tricky about it at all. On one side, there is a "package" of financial safety and security, FREEDOM from active worry and "market watcher anxiety", "set it and forget it" investment, and guaranteed monthly income of a known, certain amount, that you can't outlive. That's the 'product'. We help you choose the best of these "products" for your personal Freedom Protection Plan. On the other side, there's YOU, the "customer". You buy the product for its collection of benefits – unique exclusive benefits not matched by any other investment.

Now, let's talk about why annuities are so safe.

Over the past 100 years, retail investors including retirees have <u>lost</u> trillions of dollars in stock market crashes, individual stock companies' bankruptcies (like: General Motors, Sears, Bed, Bath & Beyond), collapsed mutual funds, even savings-and-loan and bank failures. Many people hold mutual funds, ETF's, pension accounts and don't even know what stocks are in them! Lately, the government has pressured fund managers to invest in "green new deal" stocks proving to be very high risk. Some retirees make the mistake of relying entirely on their past employer's pension fund only to see their pension income suddenly slashed by 25%, even 50%. With one such famous case, in Ohio, pensions were cut in half, and it took almost 6 years of litigation and an Act of Congress to get them restored.

Real estate can be almost as risky. Look at the "mass migration" that has recently occurred, from crime-plagued cities that were once ideal places to invest and from high tax states, to Florida, Texas, and Tennessee. If an investor had his money "locked up" in real estate in the wrong places at this time, he was in trouble!

In those same 100 years, <u>no</u> annuity income has stopped. Everyone with guaranteed lifetime income from annuities has been paid as agreed.

Here's why…

Unlike banks, life insurance companies, by design, are NOT highly leveraged. In the 2008 Wall Street & Bank crash, Bear Stearns and Lehman Brothers were extremely highly leveraged with paper thin capital reserves, as were 386 banks, and they all failed. Even as AIG's banking business crashed, its life insurance company stayed solvent and could not be raided to pay debts of its insolvent bank! Its annuity payments were never stopped. More recently, a giant Silicon Valley Bank failed and triggered several other bank failures. During all this, no company backing annuities had the same fate.

By their corporate charters and by law, insurance companies cannot wildly speculate with their customers' principal funds. All other investments feature speculation.

Life insurance companies are federally AND state regulated. Most states even backstop some annuity commitments, in somewhat the same way banks have FDIC backing. In total, life insurance companies are the most highly regulated, most watch-dog-ed financial institutions!

By using the safety of large numbers, life insurance companies have their risks spread over all policyholders. Their success at this kind of 'financial engineering' is unmatched. Warren Buffet has often said that no business matches the upside and safety of insurance companies. Annuities are "over-built" for safety, much like Amish construction of bedroom furniture or barns is over-built to last generations. Even giant companies have de-risked their pensions by buying billion-dollar annuities. And top pro athletes are urged to buy annuities to prevent "blowing all their money" and to guarantee income after their playing days are over.

Annuities are the "steady Eddie". Throughout markets' ups and downs, from the Great Depression to 2008 to now, throughout bad recessions (like the Carter years) to sky-high inflation (the Carter and Biden years), throughout war and peace, THE "steady Eddie" never giving into trouble has been: annuities. Its support of Guaranteed Income For Life has never failed.

Now, here's a word to the wise...

One of the great "fathers" of the guaranteed income strategy, Barry James Dyke, author of Pirates of Manhattan, a 30-year financial professional and Wall Street insider said this after the 2008 crash: "After the greatest financial crisis since the Great Depression, Wall Street continues to speculate with your retirement savings with reckless abandon. Only a Guaranteed Income Strategy can create the risk-free retirement income you deserve."

## Now...Do Only "Unsophisticated" Investors Buy Annuities?

Dan S. Kennedy is the author of 36 business books including The No B.S. Guide to Selling Your Company for Top Dollar and The No B.S. Guide to Wealth Attraction for Entrepreneurs, and a popular advisor to small business owners. He says: "I am wealthy and a fairly sophisticated investor with diversified holdings in public and private companies, ETF's, corporate notes and real estate. But I still have a collection of annuities, as the solid foundation, guaranteeing me an excellent retirement income for life. Even if other investments were wiped out, I have that guaranteed income that cannot be reduced or taken away. The interest rates are comparable or superior to CD's and T-bills, but nothing else guarantees certain income for life. Frankly, I get kidded about being a "scaredy-cat" or "grandmother investor" by some of my friends and peers discussing investing, but I don't care. To my mind, a certain guaranteed income is a sensible, smart piece of investment strategy even if you are a multi-millionaire – and if you are of more modest means, even more important."

Friend…there is Nothing Like The Freedom Protection Plan!

At Wealth Express® we have made it our mission to more thoroughly understand the entire annuities market better than anyone, in order to use these great financial tools to create PERSONALIZED Guaranteed Income For Life for each individual or husband and wife couple we serve. If anybody knows more about this than we do, we'd like to meet them!

When you have YOUR Freedom Protection Plan in place, you can finally RELAX ABOUT MONEY. There's just nothing else that can provide that.

And remember, YOUR Freedom Protection Plan can be created for you with NO COST, NO OBLIGATION and NEVER, EVER, EVER ANY SALES PRESSURE. Our Wealth Express® Certified Advisor, whom you'll meet with, must sign our Integrity Pledge and meet definitive qualifications. No one is every "judgmental" about your finances. If, for example, you have "scattered investments" bought at different times from different sources, you're not alone! If you are at risk without fully understanding it, you are not alone! We are here to help you get it all organized, under firm control, and SIMPLIFIED. Your discussion with us is absolutely private and confidential.

## Call 833-600-2832 now

## to schedule your FREE Retirement Risk Assessment Meeting with a Wealth Express® Certified Advisor.

*WSA 125*

# 10

## Why You Can Be Certain (with Guaranteed Income For Life)

You can feel confident in Guaranteed Investment For Life for several solid reasons, and the biggest one is because an insurance company backs it.

You and a reliable insurance company signed a contract. They are legally obliged to guarantee your return and your regular checks...Of course, the paper's only as good as the company that signs it. But here we're talking about big insurance companies. The kinds of companies specializing in making money, never losing it. Decades of sustainable wisdom are normal; these are not start-ups with an unproven business model, and their business is all about YOUR security.

## Financial Reliability

Insurance companies are well-capitalized and regulated entities with strong financial reserves. This stability assures that the insurance company can fulfill its financial obligations, including guaranteeing the principal and interest payments associated with Guaranteed Investment For Life.

## Risk Mitigation

Guaranteed Income For Life offers principal protection, meaning that the insurer guarantees the return on your initial investment, regardless of market performance. This protection helps mitigate investment risk and provides peace of mind, especially during market volatility.

## Regulatory Oversight

Insurance companies are subject to rigorous regulatory oversight by state insurance departments, which helps ensure compliance with solvency requirements and consumer protection standards. This regulatory framework adds an extra layer of security for your Guaranteed Income For Life investment, meaning you will never worry about when your monthly retirement paycheck will arrive.

## Longevity Protection

Insurance companies specialize in managing longevity risk, which is the risk of outliving one's savings. Guaranteed Income For Life provides you with a solid income stream for as long as you live that can help you manage this risk and maintain financial security throughout retirement.

## Guaranteed Benefits

Guaranteed Income For Life can be set up with optional riders or features offering additional benefits, such as guaranteed minimum withdrawal benefits (GMWB) or enhanced death benefits. These tools work on your behalf to further enhance your fund's value proposition and provide additional security.

You can be certain you will have the money you need every month. You will know exactly how much your income will be. You can budget around it. You can retire around it and enjoy your golden years to the fullest!

After years of uncertainty, stress, and the rat race...this is the downshift you've been waiting and counting on, hoping and praying for.

# 11

## Why Your Guaranteed Income For Life Can't Be Snatched Away

The principal investment and earnings of your Guaranteed Income For Life investment are protected from loss due to several key features. And your Wealth Express® Certified Advisor is ready to show you exactly how this works. Your Advisor will be your greatest ally as you plan your retirement and get the Guaranteed Income For Life that you deserve.

Your Advisor is an experienced, highly vetted, well-trained financial professional with only your best interest in mind. They are caring, patient, competent experts who have seen and heard it all and know the ins and outs of the journey. You'll want to meet with your Advisor because they have advised hundreds of people who, like you, want a safe, secure, sane retirement—and when you meet them you can be rest assured they will answer any question you may have. Your Advisor will even know about questions you haven't even considered, and will make that part of the process—no stone is left unturned, no topic is untouched, so you are fully educated and equipped with Guaranteed Income For Life.

## Principal Protection

Guaranteed Income For Life guarantees principal protection, ensuring that the initial investment amount is safeguarded from market downturns or investment losses. This means that regardless of how the underlying investments perform, your fund's principal investment remains intact, and your monthly income stream is never interrupted. Imagine how that security will feel when others are burning up their days trying to beat the market on their own.

## Guaranteed Interest Rate

Guaranteed Income For Life often comes with a guaranteed minimum interest rate, ensuring that the fund will earn a minimum level of interest over time. This provides a floor of protection for your fund's earnings, even during a low market returns or economic uncertainty. How reassuring is that!

## Insurance Backing

Insurance companies, regulated entities with strong financial reserves, typically issue Guaranteed Income For Life plans. The insurer's backing provides an additional layer of security for you, because as I mentioned, insurance companies are required to maintain adequate capital reserves to fulfill their financial obligations, including guaranteeing fund payments.

## Contractual Obligations

Guaranteed Income For Life is governed by a contractual agreement between you and the insurance company. The terms of the fund's contract specify the rights and obligations of both parties, including the guarantee of principal protection and the terms of any income payments. These contractual obligations ensure that your rights are legally protected and enforceable.

## Long-Term Commitment

Guaranteed Income For Life is designed to provide long-term financial security and income in retirement. Your plan is structured to withstand market fluctuations and economic downturns, ensuring that you can rely on receiving your fund payments for the duration of the contract term.

Overall, the combination of principal protection, guaranteed interest rates, insurance backing, contractual obligations, and long-term commitment makes it so unlikely that the principal investment and earnings of Guaranteed Income For Life can be snatched away…it can actually legally be called "Guaranteed". Because it is.

With this…your retirement is LOCKED IN. And your RETIREMENT IDENTITY will remain pure, preserved. What do I mean by retirement identity? I mean…we all have some idea or how we envision ourselves during retirement. Who do you see yourself being in retirement? The loving grandparent who spends time with the kids? An artist? A gardener? Whether you have put a little or a lot of time into thinking about it, you probably have some idea of who you would like to be in retirement. And that is vitally important. Nearly all financial companies get this wrong. They ask, "How much money do you have?" You ask, "will it be enough?" You can't answer that question yet. Because you don't know how much money you'll need until you know who you want to be in retirement.

**Call 833-600-2832 now**

**to schedule your FREE Retirement Risk Assessment Meeting with a Wealth Express® Certified Advisor.**

*WSA 126*

# 12

## The Benefit of Certainty…How Guaranteed Income For Life Can Make Retirement Worry-Free, Stress-Free

- Think how much easier your life will be.

- No watching, wondering, or worrying about the market.

- No cutting back on your lifestyle.

- Being able to travel / stay active / live / retire AS YOU IMAGINED IT.

A quick question: If you had to pick between the journey and the destination, which would it be?

Yes, your work life and career have been amazing. You made the most of it—no matter how much dense underbrush you had to clear.

Some days the journey was a joy, others not so much. Everyone can justify a preference for the journey or the destination. Some say, "The journey is how we get there, and we love it!" and others say, "Yes, but the journey means nothing without a destination."

Think about it this way: What if there was NO DESTINATION, only the endless journey?

Would you pay the price to excel at football if you only had grueling practices in the scorching heat, punishing tackling drills, and endless uphill wind sprints? With no games or playoffs or wins?

Would you love watching a movie with no ending? With just scene after scene—and no stirring finale where the hero takes the day?

Now, continue the thought experiment and imagine it's two years from your retirement date.

You've planned for your golden years; the destination is almost in sight. Yes!!

Now here's the twist…

What if, in the blink of an eye, you could fast-forward to your dream retirement destination, right now? How much would you miss your work life journey? Nada, right?

**Your retirement is exciting because it will be here sooner than you realize!**

With Guaranteed Income For Life…you've already crafted a fantastic financial retirement plan and ensured you're getting a solid paycheck every month. But remember, your retirement financial plan is your transportation; it is not the destination.

So, what then? It's time to begin planning the new vistas you'll get to enjoy.

What will your dream retirement actually look like? What will be your RETIREMENT IDENTITY? How will you spend your days of newfound freedom?

It's easy to get lost in thoughts of sleeping in every day or spending significant time chilling on beach chairs. Once you are well-rested and sun-drenched, the possibilities are still exciting. You probably already have some great ideas for filling your retirement days. Here are a few fun options to consider:

**Master Your Favorite Hobby**

Now, you can golf on weekdays, and sand traps are no longer a mystery. A couple of refresher lessons with the pro and some extra practice time to finally solve that problem!

Then there is getting together with the gang...maybe they're old friends, and the fishing is now so good that you almost feel like a semi-pro and are having more fun than ever.

Maybe you love painting or pottery? Time to get those new natural brushes you've always wanted, or the XL Pro wheel you've always needed. Or if you love woodworking, you can finally make that artisan sideboard table with your new smooth-running bandsaw. And now you have time to cultivate an award-winning garden, so nice it will look better than the grounds of the Biltmore. Welcome to the endless hobby world, where you unleash your inner fulfillment quest!

## Relocate to a Dream Destination

You've always loved everything about Puerto Vallarta, so you've moved south of the border and have a whole crop of vibrant and exciting new friends. Picture it: your morning starts LATE with no rush at all. Then you have a quick swim, a relaxing lunch, and why not a nap? Then...it's time for the books you love, Margaritaville, and more endless summer! Or it may be this isn't you at all. Everyone is different. Everyone's retirement needs and desires are different. But EVERYONE'S retirement nightmare is the same: Running out of money.

## Spend Time with Family

The internet and your Facebook feed are full of other people saying things like "If we'd known that grandkids were so much fun, we would've have had them much sooner!" They make you feel young again, and there's nothing better than meeting your kid's baby. Now it is your turn to belong like never before, create new memories, help your kids, and download your wisdom and love to the next generation.

## Travel

You can finally take that extended Alaskan cruise, travel around the US, or visit the South of France for five whole weeks (every year!) like you've always wanted. Some folks just throw a dart at a map and visit the random locations they hit. All the discoveries, new foods, new friends, culture, and language await you!

## Remodel

When you plan to stay home in your golden years, you'll have time for those compelling renovation projects you've always dreamed about. The 8" crown molding the builder should have installed in the first place will look fantastic, and that master bath upgrade you've always wanted will make your mornings even better once you get it done exactly as you wanted. You will have so much fun and new pro skills Bob Villa will call for advice.

## Start a Business

Have you always wanted to take a shot at starting your dream side hustle? After all, you know you can build a far better acoustic guitar than what's out there, especially with all the innovations you've come up with! Or maybe your deep knowledge and work experience are incredibly valuable, so you get into coaching and consulting, but you do it the way YOU want to. Now you'll have time to go for it and make it happen!

## Volunteer

Perhaps you've always loved a particular cause or charitable organization, and you've not had enough time to make the significant difference you wanted to. Now you'll be able to rock the volunteer world and help others as you've always dreamed.

## Do a Whole Lotta Nothing

There is nothing wrong with just maintaining your lifestyle. For you, this might be your dream retirement, because you LOVE peace and quiet. After years of the grind, commuting, dealing with customers and clients, a bazillion meetings, too many 11-hour days, and relentless deadlines, the simple life is good!

None of this happens unless your retirement is secure and you have retirement income that doesn't cut into your working capital and your ability to enjoy the discretionary spending for the fun things you've always wanted. Guaranteed Income For Life makes this happen for you.

Whatever your dream retirement looks like, it has a better chance of happening with Guaranteed Income For Life.

# 13

## Why "Spend Down Die Broke" DOESN'T WORK

The "Spend Down Die Broke" theory suggests that spending all your assets during retirement is the way to go. The idea is to leave nothing behind. As easy and convenient as this sounds, it may not be a solid financial strategy for multiple reasons.

## Unforeseen Expenses

You know that life is unpredictable. Unexpected expenses such as big healthcare costs or long-term care needs can arise during retirement. Mindlessly spending all your assets without preserving a financial cushion can leave you vulnerable to financial hardship later in life.

## Legacy Planning

Many wish to leave a financial legacy for their loved ones or charitable causes. The "Spend Down Die Broke" approach does not align with these intentions. It will destroy your ability to leave behind a meaningful inheritance or support future generations.

## Longevity Risk

With increasing life expectancy, retirees face the risk of outliving their savings. Exhausting all your assets early in retirement may leave you without sufficient resources to support yourself later, especially if you live longer than anticipated. That should be a GOOD thing, not a bad thing. But in this modern world, where basic living has been booby-trapped with a hair-trigger so nearly every move you make costs money, you need to know that you'll <u>never run out of money</u>.

## Market Volatility

Relying solely on spending down assets—without considering investment returns or market fluctuations—can leave you highly vulnerable to market downturn risks. In that case, you're practically begging for something terrible to happen. Maintaining a diversified investment portfolio and incorporating sustainable withdrawal strategies can help mitigate these risks. IF you manage your money wisely. IF you secure your lifetime income with Guaranteed Income For Life.

When developing a retirement income strategy, it's essential to carefully evaluate financial goals, risk tolerance, and lifestyle preferences.

With Guaranteed Income For Life and the expert help of your Certified Advisor, all of these issues are handled and completely mitigated. The stress-free retirement that you've always wanted will be a reality. Because you will have done the wise planning and created a CERTAIN path to the good times and peace of mind you deserve. Your retirement will be the most enjoyable, satisfying life that is POSSIBLE!

# 14

## Evaluating Your Retirement Readiness

Okay, so here are some important questions to ask yourself. And it is time to be truly candid with yourself—so no cheating, only honest answers.

When planning for retirement, several key factors should be carefully considered. All of these matter, and as you review them you'll quickly see how Guaranteed Income For Life plays a vital role for each category. This is not cookie cutter, because it is YOUR Retirement Identity we are talking about – nobody else's!

## Financial Goals

You'll want to define your retirement lifestyle goals, including expenses for housing, healthcare, travel, hobbies, and other activities. Establishing clear financial objectives will help guide your retirement planning process.

## Retirement Age

Determine the age at which you plan to retire. Consider income sources and personal preferences for timing your retirement.

## Income Sources

It is crucial to identify all potential sources of retirement income, including Social Security benefits, pension plans, retirement savings accounts (e.g., 401(k), IRA), rental income, and part-time employment). You must evaluate the reliability and sustainability of each income stream. When you add a Guaranteed Income For Life monthly retirement paycheck to your monthly social security income plus your dividend or portfolio earnings…wow! You have diverse money sources coming in every month just like when you were working! Only now, you're taking it easy. Instead of working you're doing EXACTLY what YOU want to do.

## Expenses and Budgeting

Estimate your retirement expenses based on your desired lifestyle and anticipated needs. Consider housing costs, healthcare expenses, insurance premiums, taxes, travel, and discretionary spending. Develop a budget to align your expenses with your income sources. Of course this all becomes MUCH EASIER with a Guaranteed Income For Life plan, because you'll have that retirement paycheck in your mailbox, right on time like clockwork, every single month. You'll be CERTAIN about how much money you have coming in.

## Healthcare Costs

Plan for healthcare expenses, including insurance premiums, out-of-pocket costs, and long-term care needs. To mitigate healthcare-related financial risks, explore options for Medicare coverage, supplemental insurance, health savings accounts (HSAs), and long-term care insurance.

## Investment Strategy

You'll want to develop an investment strategy tailored to your retirement goals, risk tolerance, and time horizon. It will be important to consider factors such as asset allocation, diversification, risk management, and investment expenses. Of course it's crucial to regularly review and adjust your investment portfolio as needed to align with changing circumstances and market conditions.

## Tax Planning

You'll always want to keep tax planning as a priority. You'll love the results when you implement tax-advantaged strategies to maximize your retirement income and minimize tax liabilities. Guaranteed Income For Life is one of the fantastic ways to save on taxes.

## Estate Planning

Developing an estate plan is crucial to ensure the efficient transfer of assets to heirs and beneficiaries, no matter what stage you are in. Consider wills, trusts, beneficiary designations, powers of attorney, healthcare directives, and legacy planning goals. With the help of your Certified Advisor, you can dial in your estate plan so your family and future generations receive your assets just as you intend.

## Your Wealth Express® Certified Advisor

Consider consulting with a Wealth Express® Certified Advisor to help you navigate the complexities of retirement planning, optimize your financial resources, and achieve your retirement goals.

Why am I suggesting this? You've heard me rave about Guaranteed Income For Life plans and retirement paychecks and all the things I love about this, an essential retirement tool. But frankly...you'll get the juicy ins and outs of the plan from your Wealth Express® Certified Advisor. They're the experts who can sit with you, listen to your concerns, hopes, and dreams, consider your existing resources, and show you the full opportunity and solution. DON'T JUST TAKE MY WORD FOR IT. Speak to an advisor. The meeting is free. There's no obligation to get a plan if it doesn't feel right. Let them help you explore the possibilities.

By carefully considering these key factors and developing a comprehensive retirement plan, you can better prepare for a financially secure and fulfilling retirement.

## Assessing Your Current Financial Situation And Retirement Goals

Assessing your current financial situation and retirement goals with your Wealth Express® Certified Advisors involves several key steps. With their expert help, this is how you MAKE RETIREMENT PLANNING EASY. With their proven insights, there is no more wondering, worrying, and guessing. No more need to constantly watch market trends and spike your blood pressure.

### Identify Retirement Goals

Your Advisor will help you clarify your retirement goals and aspirations. You'll consider factors such as your desired retirement age, lifestyle preferences, housing preferences, travel plans, healthcare needs, and legacy objectives—your RETIREMENT IDENTITY! It will be fun to get specific about what you envision for your retirement years.

## How Guaranteed Income For Life Can Meet Your Specific Retirement Needs

Your Freedom Protection Plan featuring a Guaranteed Income For Life can help meet your financial needs in retirement in several ways.

## Principal Protection

Guaranteed Income For Life offers total principal protection, ensuring that your initial investment is safeguarded from market downturns. When everyone's watching and worrying, you'll be…???...when your friends are 70 and filling out applications for menial part-time jobs, you'll be…??? Knowing that your retirement savings are protected from significant losses can provide peace of mind and financial security.

## Potential For Growth

While providing principal protection, Guaranteed Income For Life also offers the potential for growth linked to the performance of an underlying market index, such as the S&P 500. This allows you to participate in market gains up to a certain cap or limit, providing the opportunity to grow your retirement savings over time.

Consider this…there are giant marble-faced bank skyscrapers in every American metropolis for a good reason: ENDLESS FEES. If you want to protect your savings with zero return, you may be better off stuffing it under your mattress or burying it in the backyard. BUT know better, because you HAVE TO invest so your money can make you more money if you're going to stay afloat for the rest of your life. A Guaranteed Income For Life plan gives you that and comes with iron-clad promises you can count on.

## Guaranteed Minimum Interest Rate

Even in years when the underlying index performs poorly, Guaranteed Income For Life offers a guaranteed minimum interest rate. This ensures that your funds will earn a minimum level of interest, providing certainty, stability, and predictability to your retirement income. You'll say goodbye to all those stomach aches from stressing over every little market downturn.

## Tax-Deferred Growth

Guaranteed Income For Life offers tax-deferred growth, meaning you won't pay taxes on you withdraw. This can help maximize the growth potential of your retirement savings, allowing your money to compound over time without the drag of annual taxes.

When you consider the earring potential PLUS the tax savings, your Guaranteed Income For Life plan essentially GROWS from the fixed return percentage you agree to when you enroll in the plan (basically, just because your plan calls for 4%-

5% growth, you are, in a way, earning more than that because of the tax savings).

## Lifetime Income Options

Many Guaranteed Income For Life plans offer optional riders or features that allow you to convert your fund into a stream of lifetime monthly income payments. This can provide a reliable source of income to supplement Social Security benefits and other retirement income streams, helping you meet your ongoing living expenses in retirement. NOW…budgeting is easier. Planning is easier. LIFE IS EASIER.

## Legacy Planning

Guaranteed Income For Life can also be used as a legacy planning strategy to leave a financial legacy for your loved ones or charitable causes. You can designate beneficiaries to receive any remaining fund value upon your death, providing an inheritance for future generations. Your Wealth Express® Certified Advisor is also an expert at legacy planning, and can share fantastic strategies you probably never considered.

Overall, Guaranteed Income For Life can be a valuable tool for meeting your retirement financial needs by offering a combination of principal protection, growth potential, tax advantages, and income certainty.

Guaranteed Income For Life fast-tracks all of this.

# 15

# Making the Most of Your Retirement Savings

## Strategies for maximizing your retirement income...

Guaranteed Income For Life offers tremendous benefits for your retirement planning; You'll enjoy safety, security, certainty, having zero risk, principal protection, tax savings, monthly income, guaranteed returns, legacy provision, and income diversity, just to mention a few of them. The best way to maximize retirement income will depend on your circumstances and goals. Here are some reasons why Guaranteed Income For Life can be advantageous to your retirement income plan.

## The role of Guaranteed Income For Life in preserving your principal...

A Guaranteed Income For Life plan preserves your principal through a combination of features designed to protect your initial investment from market downturns:

### Principal Guarantee

Principal protection is one of the primary features of a Guaranteed Income For Life plan. This means that regardless of how the underlying market index performs, your initial investment is shielded from any losses. Even if the index experiences negative returns, your principal amount remains intact. Imagine how that will feel when your friends stare at their investing charts with all arrows pointing south.

## Minimum Interest Rate Guarantee

Guaranteed Income For Life typically comes with a guaranteed minimum interest rate. This ensures that even if the performance of the underlying index is poor or negative, your investment will still earn a minimum level of interest. This feature provides an iron-clad floor of protection for your investment, safeguarding against the possibility of earning no returns.

Overall, Guaranteed Income For Life offers principal protection, minimum interest rate guarantees, and market swing protections to help safeguard your initial investment from market fluctuations. These features provide you with peace of mind and financial security, making Guaranteed Income For Life a wise choice if you like balancing growth potential and risk mitigation in your retirement savings strategy.

## Tips for managing withdrawals and ensuring a steady income stream...

I've learned the importance of adequately managing withdrawals firsthand—from hearing all the 'I wish I had known this' stories of so many retirees.

Suppose you want to ensure a steady income stream and safeguard your financial security in retirement. In that case, it's important to have a well-planned withdrawal strategy, also known as a decumulation strategy. That's because choosing the best way to access and spend your retirement savings will help you get the most out of it. You'll avoid paying unnecessary taxes and running out of money.

There are many methods for withdrawing retirement savings, and no single approach is right for everyone. Most financial professionals agree it's a good idea to combine them. So that's where the expert wisdom of your Wealth Express® Certified Advisor will come in handy.

The best way to avoid unnecessary withdrawals from a Guaranteed Income For Life plan to ensure a steady stream of income is to utilize the plan's built-in features for converting your plan into a reliable source of lifetime income. Here's how you can achieve this:

### Annual Regular Income

Consider setting up your Guaranteed Income For Life plan to convert the plan contract into a series of guaranteed lifetime income payments. This process typically involves selecting a payout option, such as a life plan or a period-certain plan, which provides a stream of income for your lifetime or a specified period, respectively.

## Income Riders

Many Guaranteed Income For Life plans offer optional income riders or features that allow you to convert your plan into a stream of guaranteed lifetime income payments without changing the contract. These income riders typically provide enhanced benefits, such as higher withdrawal percentages or cost-of-living adjustments, in exchange for an additional fee.

## Systematic Withdrawal Plans

If you prefer more flexibility in managing your retirement income, your Certified Advisor can help you set up a systematic withdrawal from your Guaranteed Income For Life plan. This involves withdrawing a predetermined amount of money from your plan at regular intervals, such as monthly or annually, to supplement your other sources of retirement income.

## Wait For Maturity

Some Guaranteed Income For Life plans have a maturity date at which point you can receive a lump sum payment or convert the plan into a stream of income. By waiting until maturity, you can avoid withdrawals during the accumulation phase and ensure a steady income stream during retirement. Your Certified Advisor can help dial that just right in for you.

Your Guaranteed Income For Life plan can play a valuable role in a comprehensive retirement plan by providing guaranteed income to cover essential living expenses throughout retirement. Here's how it fits beautifully into your plan.

**Stable Income Stream**

Guaranteed Income For Life offers a reliable and predictable source of income that can help cover essential living expenses, such as housing, healthcare, and groceries. By converting a portion of your retirement savings into your plan of choice, you can create a stable income stream for your lifetime or a specified period, providing financial security and peace of mind.

CERTAINTY. DEAD SOLID CERTAINTY. You earned it. Now you'll get it…

**Longevity Protection**

One of the primary benefits of Guaranteed Income For Life is longevity protection, which guards against the risk of outliving your savings.

This plan provides guaranteed lifetime income payments, regardless of how long you live, ensuring you won't run out of money in retirement, even if you live well into your 90s or beyond.

### Risk Management

Guaranteed Income For Life helps manage various retirement risks, including market volatility, inflation, and sequence of returns risk. By transferring the risk of investment performance and longevity to the insurer, this plan provides certainty and stability to your retirement income, regardless of economic conditions or market fluctuations.

### Tax Efficiency

Guaranteed Income For Life offers tax-deferred growth, meaning you won't pay taxes on your earnings until you receive income payments. This can help optimize your retirement income by allowing your money to grow tax-free during the accumulation phase, potentially reducing your tax burden in retirement.

Are you seeing the big picture? Are you jazzed about how great it looks? You'll have the certainty you deserve, your money worries will disappear, you'll waste zero time stressing about the markets, your custom-crafted RETIREMENT IDENTITY is a reality you'll enjoy—every single day of your life, even if you live to 100!

Overall, Guaranteed Income For Life can be an essential component of a comprehensive retirement plan, providing a reliable source of income, longevity protection, risk management, diversification, and tax efficiency to support your financial needs and goals in retirement.

# 16

## The Magic Of Income Diversity

In rapidly changing economic times and constantly shifting landscapes, relying on a single income source is too risky. Building multiple income streams is something that you will appreciate in the long run. To create improved financial stability, prepare for unexpected expenses, or work toward your long-term goals. Diversifying your revenue sources will boost your financial resilience. Relying on your W-2 income alone ties your financial well-being to just one source. This makes you vulnerable to economic downturns, job loss, or sector-specific challenges. Diversifying your income sources helps create a buffer to shield you from unforeseen setbacks. Failure to create multiple income streams is one of the biggest mistakes people can make. Guaranteed Income For Life boosts your income diversity. It's a strategy that works while you are still working. And you'll love how it works even better when you've retired.

For example, if you have Guaranteed Income For Life PLUS your Social Security income PLUS dividends and your other investments that bring you money…put them together and you have true income diversity.

### Types of Income Streams

Your main job serves as the foundation for your income structure. Yes, you give it your full effort every day, but you must not ONLY rely on these 9-to-5 wages. This income is a basis and provides a measure of security, but relying on it is too risky.

### Side Hustles

Side gigs or part-time ventures can supplement your primary income from your day job, and provide extra cash to invest or meet your overall income goals.

## Investments

Income from investments like stocks, bonds, real estate, or dividends is a great way to increased overall income.

## Freelancing or Consulting

When you have specific skills, freelancing or consulting can be an outstanding source of extra income.

## Online Business Ventures

E-commerce, blogging, and offering membership-based subscriptions to online courses are fantastic options for generating additional income.

## Passive Income

This income stream involves earning money with little or no hands-on effort, via royalty payments, affiliate marketing, and rent collection.

## The Benefits Of Multiple Income Streams

So what are the benefits of having additional income streams? Here are just a few:

You gain true stability and flexibility because

you have other options if one income source fails. This helps to reduce the impact of any financial setbacks. Plus, you'll find you're nimbler when circumstances change or new opportunities arise.

Extra cash flow is helpful because it provides added funds to invest, save, or put toward professional or personal growth. Building multiple income streams helps unleash your inner entrepreneur. This mindset can foster improved creativity and innovation in any endeavor.

OR…you could simply add your Guaranteed Income For Life retirement paycheck to the Social Security you already paid into! Boom! Easy. Done. Time to relax, never worry, and enjoy the good days ahead!

## Strategies For Creating Multiple Income Streams

The first step is to take inventory. Realistically assess your skills, interests, and expertise to determine your possible approaches. Also, the time and energy you have available to devote to your new ventures is crucial. Don't overreach, and don't hesitate to begin small. You don't need to launch 10 new ventures, as exciting as that might seem! Instead, start with one additional income source (OK, maybe two if you are superhuman!).

Networking is super-valuable when starting a new income stream. Your personal and professional contacts are a honeypot of wisdom and insight regarding new income-generating possibilities. If you've never networked before, you can be sure most people will love to tell you about themselves and what they know to help you get going.

Building multiple income streams isn't merely a financial strategy. This diversification mindset can help you gain improved stability, fresh perspective, and added flexibility, and boost your personal growth. In a constantly changing world, having multiple income streams gives you a cushion. You'll weather financial storms, handle opportunities that come your way, and go after your goals with improved confidence. You'll love taking a proactive approach to creating new income streams because it positions you for greater financial resilience and success.

### Call 833-600-2832 now

### to schedule your FREE Retirement Risk Assessment Meeting with a Wealth Express® Certified Advisor.

*WSA 128*

# 17

## WHAT IF...you DON'T get a Guaranteed Income For Life Plan?

Let's think about an alternative financial retirement plan scenario. One where you've made some plans but don't include Guaranteed Income For Life. So what will your dream retirement look like in this case?

First, forget about sleeping in every day or

chilling on your favorite beach. Regular rest and sun will just have to wait until summer weekends, and that's only if you're not on the clock at your big-box store part-time job. Your other great ideas for filling your retirement days will have to wait a while, too.

## What About Your Favorite Hobby?

Weekend golf might still be an option…if you can afford it. Sand traps will remain a mystery, and you'll have to live with your same old handicap. No time for lessons with the pro. You'll hopefully get together with the gang…those old dear friends. But those outings will be far less frequent than you've hoped for—and that's if you have the budget for it. Oh, and painters, those new natural brushes must remain on the wish list. And pottery making will be fun, but only at an occasional free class at the community center. Woodworking will remain a passion; you'll only dream of the tools you need, like a new bandsaw. Cultivating an award-winning garden will be out of the question because you won't have time to get it right (your part-time job, or two, will crowd out almost all your free time). Your hobbies will be there, but you'll still be hoping to do more of them…someday….when will you find time to enjoy them if you have to work or worry about money?

## Relocate (This Was The Plan, But Not Now)

Moving south of the border like you've always wanted and engaging with friends who are already enjoying it won't be on your vista. No lazy morning starts, and certainly no sleeping in. A swim at the local YMCA but no hopping out of bed for a quick plunge into the Gulf of Mexico. How about a relaxing lunch every day and a nap? Nope. You won't have any budget for this. There will be some time for the books you love from the local library, but far less Margaritaville time. And no endless summer—you'll be able to catch the rays you love only if you can afford to travel to your favorite sunspot.

## Spend Less Time With Family

You'll be jealous of friends constantly talking on Facebook about how their grandkids make them feel so young again, and about how there's nothing better than meeting their kid's baby, blah, blah, blah. Because you won't have the freedom to be there for YOUR family nearly as often as you'd like. Sure, there will be new holiday memories, but you won't be able to help your kids and mind your grandchildren at the drop of a hat. There will be times to download wisdom and love, but far fewer—and more often than not, on FaceTime, not in person.

## Travel Won't Be An Option

The extended Alaskan cruise will have to wait. Traveling around the US, or visiting the South of France…well, the same. You can pretty much forget about visiting random destinations on a whim. You might be able to explore some local destinations if there is weekend time, or enjoy a staycation, and that's a big maybe—because don't forget about your part-time job bagging groceries most Saturdays and Sundays. All the dream discoveries, the new foods, and new friends will be greatly reduced.

## Remodel, Some Day?

When staying home in your golden years, you'll hopefully be able to afford the upkeep. The 8" premium crown molding you've always wanted will not be affordable. That master bath upgrade you've always wanted is simply out of the question. Hopefully, you'll be able to use your skills to repair the plumbing in your house or gain the skills needed to do the work because hiring a plumber is not in the cards either.

## Do Not Start a Business

Starting your dream side hustle will be fun to think about, but that will be it—you won't have the working capital to invest. Your deep knowledge and work experience are incredibly valuable, so maybe you'll get into coaching and consulting if they don't think your skills are outdated. But you'll need to take any work that comes your way, even projects you don't believe in because you'll need the money.

## Volunteer Less

Yes, you've always loved your favorite cause or charitable organization. Without Guaranteed Income For Life you won't have enough time to make the significant difference as you've hoped. You'll be able to volunteer, but not nearly at the level that you've always dreamed.

## Do More Work & Rest Far Less

Maintaining your lifestyle might be much harder than you've hoped for. For you, now an abundance of peace you've always wanted might not be in reach. The simple life might still be elusive because you'll likely need to keep working and hustling to make ends meet.

Do you see what's happening here? Since you've not included Guaranteed Income For Life in your retirement plan, your capacity to enjoy your desired retirement lifestyle choices will be far more limited. The odds of ever living your dream retirement become very low at best.

**Call 833-600-2832 now**

**to schedule your FREE Retirement Risk Assessment Meeting with a Wealth Express® Certified Advisor.**

*WSA 129*

# 18

## The Mindset For Thriving In Uncertainty

Maintaining a positive mindset during financial uncertainty is crucial for your overall well-being. Here are five tips to help you stay positive:

### You Can Control This.

You are human, and it's expected to have some

anxiety about finances in uncertain times. Your trouble detectors go off for good reasons during uncertain times, so it's worth being aware of the dangers. How about considering this approach: Instead of dwelling on factors beyond your control, focus on what you can do to improve your financial situation. On your way to your dream retirement, this might include adhering to a budget, reducing expenses, increasing savings, liquidating assets you no longer need, or exploring new income opportunities. When you do your review work, try doing it in a soothing place. Guaranteed Income For Life gives you built-in control, certainty, and a solid financial basis—regardless of what the times might throw down. Your guaranteed monthly paycheck is immune to market fluctuations.

Complaining about bad things happening is part of life. We all do it. A certain amount of recreational complaining can be fun. However, it's easy to slip into a negative mindset. You can't control what's happening, but you can control how you think and respond. This mindset approach takes away so much worry it creates a perpetual positive feeling. By concentrating on practical steps, you'll feel empowered and more in control of your financial future.

## Practice Gratitude

How much can small moments of expressing gratitude impact your life? A lot! Experts tell us the act of practicing gratitude has a myriad of benefits. When you take time each day to reflect on what you're grateful for, the mental health impact is remarkable, regardless of your financial circumstances. Cultivating a mindset of gratitude can help shift your focus away from negativity and anxiety, promoting feelings of optimism, contentment, and well-being. Consider keeping a gratitude journal or simply making mental notes of the positive aspects of your life. Gratitude does make us better and happier!

And with Guaranteed Income For Life, you'll know you're covered...your spouse knows...your friends will know. While they're complaining, you're contemplating how to enhance your life next in your golden years and how grateful you are to have a solid plan in place.

It will be helpful to tap into the calm, professional mindset of your Wealth Express® Certified Advisor. They have seen it all: every possible facet of financial uncertainty and mayhem. They are equipped with answers and solutions you never considered or thought possible. You'll be grateful that they know how to address the goals specific to your life, your vision, and your RETIREMENT IDENTITY.

## Embracing A Growth Mindset Towards Wealth and Investment

Embracing a growth mindset regarding wealth and investment involves a commitment to continuous learning and an attitude of resilience and adaptability. You'll love how Guaranteed Income For Life reinforces your growth mindset. You'll have an extra gear (or two!) you can shift to whenever you want—a horsepower boost that others only hope for. Here's how the most successful investors cultivate a growth mindset, and you can too.

### Embrace Learning

Approach investing with a willingness to learn and grow. It's not a mistake if you've learned from it. There are tremendous paybacks when you continuously educate yourself about current financial markets, investment strategies that work, and personal finance principles.

Also, this is where your Wealth Express® Certified Advisor becomes a phenomenal ally. Because tapping into their extensive experience, wisdom, know-how, and good counsel gives you a competitive learning edge. What you'll accomplish with your world-class coach—one who knows all the ropes—will outshine anything your friends are trying to accomplish by solo learning. It's almost like you'll have a new superpower...because you will!

## View Setbacks As Opportunities

Instead of viewing setbacks, mistakes, or losses as failures, why not see them as opportunities for growth and learning? Analyzing what went wrong, identifying lessons learned, and using this knowledge to improve your investment approach going forward is powerful. Often, the sooner you embrace challenges as opportunities to strengthen your skills and resilience as an investor, the better. Yes, this is all true, but it will be fantastic to not worry about suffering losses, knowing that Guaranteed Income For Life is set-back free...it is GUARANTEED!

## The Power of Long-Term Growth

Adopting a long-term perspective toward investing and wealth accumulation is a wise, conservative approach. Actual wealth building takes time, patience, and discipline. With Guaranteed Income For Life, you'll avoid all the hassle of constantly chasing short-term gains or reacting to market fluctuations. Regarding short-term gains, one statistic you see everywhere on the internet is that 95% of day traders fail. Research suggests that the actual figure is far higher. It's best to stay focused on your long-term financial goals and investment objectives and remain committed to your investment strategy despite temporary setbacks or market volatility. With Guaranteed Income For Life, you are already there!

## Take Calculated Risks

Be willing to take calculated risks and step outside your comfort zone to pursue growth and opportunity. The secret to getting this right is simple: calculate, calculate, and then calculate. All investments carry some level of risk. By conducting thorough research, diversifying your portfolio, and maintaining a disciplined approach, you can manage risk effectively and position yourself for long-term success. Frankly, the most significant risk you can take is NOT getting your Guaranteed Income For Life plan.

By embracing a growth attitude toward wealth and investment, you can foster a mindset of continuous improvement. You'll achieve your financial goals and build long-term, generational wealth using your resilience and adaptability.

## The Emotions You're Feeling Right Now

Regardless of what you might have heard, 100% of decisions are emotional. Yes, people reason, but we all act impulsively. Emotions can significantly influence financial decisions by shaping our perceptions, attitudes, and behaviors toward money and investing. Years of fascinating research indicate that for most people's ability to understand the factors that affect their behavior and decision-making is surprisingly poor. Here are just a few factors to consider.

And remember, you won't be on your own. Your Wealth Express® Certified Advisor can explain it better than I have here…because they can ask you questions about your life and your vision for retirement…They will NOT tell you to get Guaranteed Income For Life if it is NOT suitable for you. That's why there's no risk in taking the meeting…in exploring your options. You may discover the future you've been looking for.

## Fear And Anxiety

Fear of losing money or missing out on opportunities can lead to irrational decision-making on selling investments during market downturns or avoiding risk altogether. Fear-driven behavior can result in missed opportunities for long-term growth and negatively impact investment returns. You won't have that problem with Guaranteed Income For Life because your expert Advisor will be the rock-solid sounding board you need to address the fears and make them disappear with a down-turn proof plan!

## Greed And Overconfidence

Overconfidence in one's abilities or the belief that past investment successes will continue indefinitely can lead to excessive risk-taking and speculative behavior. Overconfidence bias can result in chasing hot stocks or investing in speculative assets without due diligence. Once again, this is where the counsel of your Wealth Express® Certified Advisor will provide a trusted reality check and make sure you don't ever fall into this ditch.

## Regret and Loss Aversion

This is when you decide to avoid regretting an alternative decision in the future. What a waste of your time, money, energy, and opportunity! Because when you experience losses or failure it can lead to decision paralysis. With Guaranteed

Income For Life, you'll eliminate losses, because the plan is GUARANTEED! And your Certified Advisor will never let you go off the rails.

## Confirmation Bias

Confirmation bias is super-common and undergirds most lousy decision-making. It occurs when investors seek out information confirming their beliefs or biases while disregarding contradictory evidence. With Guaranteed Income For Life, you get a CERTAIN plan, conservatively vetted and well regulated, carefully crafted by solid, powerhouse insurance companies who only get it right. Your plan can't be derailed by any bias, whims, or guessing what might be right. You'll have GUARANTEED income! And your Certified Advisor will always keep you on track every step of the way.

# 19

## Action Plan for Financial Certainty

THERE IS GOOD NEWS! Getting the financial certainty you've always wanted does NOT have to be complicated. We demystify it. We promise to make it easy for you and your spouse to understand, verify, and feel comfortable and CERTAINTY.

Safe, secure retirement investing and

Guaranteed Income For Life planning can be smooth sailing, set up to fit your schedule, and easily accomplished with Wealth Express®. Our days are currently filled with uncertainty and are far too chaotic—who needs any more of that? We realize you DO NOT want to worry for one moment about what goes into crafting your financial plan. Rest assured, we make the process super clear, answer every question, and eliminate uncertainty. Remember, there are no silly questions—and there is never one that is too nuanced or obscure for our patient, expert Advisors.

## What To Do Next

The Next Step is for a no-fee, no obligation Retirement Risk Assessment Meeting with a Wealth Express® Certified Advisor <u>in the privacy of your home</u>. The meeting typically takes 30 minutes, about the length of a TV program.

## What To Expect From Your Private, At-Home Meeting

**1:** COURTESY, clarity and convenience!

**2**: Our Certified Advisor will QUICKLY, SIMPLY help you identify the best Freedom Protection Plan® PERSONALIZED for your and your spouse's needs

**3**: They will show you EXACTLY the amount of Guaranteed Income you can put in place, how your money can grow over time even while you receive your monthly Guaranteed Income, even the 'death benefit' paid to your chosen beneficiaries

**4:** They will ANSWER YOUR EVERY QUESTION

**5:** If you decide to put a Freedom Protection Plan® in place, they will do the required paperwork and talk you through it in plain English

## How To Schedule Your Meeting

Simply Call **1-833-600-2832**. You'll be greeted by a U.S.-based representative who will arrange your meeting with the Wealth Express® Advisor nearest you.

Rest Assured, Your Privacy Is Respected. We live in an age of "privacy destruction". Every time you try doing anything, even ordering take-out food, you are forced to add an app to your phone, your data is "mined", and God only knows where it goes and who gets it. NOTHING YOU DISCLOSE TO US in discussing the customizing of The Freedom Protection Plan® will leave the room! Do NOT Worry About "BEING SOLD". The Freedom Protection Plan® is, ultimately, a PERSONAL decision. We want you to have all the facts and we trust you to make the best decision for you and your family. There is NO "PRESSURE."

One "Caution"….

At-home Retirement Risk Assessment Meetings are limited. An Advisor has to be licensed AND qualify with Wealth Express®. Complete a Certification. It's not like any 'body' off the street can jump in here. Thus, there are a very limited number of Advisors in your area. The best way to avoid a long delay in scheduling your Meeting is to respond immediately.

## Your Privacy Is Respected, Please Rest Assured

There is a pitched battle going on now for your privacy, and it is far worse than George Orwell foresaw in the film 1984. We live in an age of widespread data insecurity and privacy destruction. Every time you buy an item online or order take-out, you must add an app to your phone. Then your data is mined, and it is used to sell targeted advertising. This happens even if you opt-out, and Lord only knows where it goes and who gets it. Think we are exaggerating? In 2018, Meta was slapped with a $5 BILLION DOLLAR fine for failing to protect user data. We promise that NOTHING YOU DISCLOSE TO US in discussing how we customize The Freedom Protection Plan® for you will leave the room!

Please Do NOT Worry About BEING SOLD

We understand that going with The Freedom Protection Plan® and how you choose to set it up is a PERSONAL decision. No matter what your situation, we want you to have all the facts and all the answers. We trust you to make the best decision for you and your family. There is NO PRESSURE.

But again…

There are a limited number of slots for scheduling at-home meetings. This is because our Advisors are helpful, skilled people who must complete their certification and hold a 2-15 License in your state AND qualify with Wealth Express®. They are experienced professional advisors, and not just a part-timer or a temp hired off the street.

As you can imagine, because of our high qualification, integrity, and experience requirements, there are a limited number of

Certified Advisors in your area, and their schedules fill up quickly. The best way to avoid a long calendar delay in setting up your meeting is to respond as soon as the ideas in this book make sense to you.

**Call 833-600-2832 now**

**to schedule your FREE Retirement Risk Assessment Meeting with a Wealth Express® Certified Advisor.**

*WSA 130*

Made in the USA
Columbia, SC
05 November 2024